DON'T BELIEVE
THE LIE

DON'T BELIEVE THE LIE

DAVIAN TALLEY

Copyright © 2021 by Davian Talley

All rights reserved. This book or any portion thereof may not be reproduced or used in any manner whatsoever without the express written permission of the publisher except for the use of brief quotations in a book review.

Limits of Liability and Disclaimer of Warranty

The author and publisher shall not be liable for your misuse of this material. This book is strictly for informational purposes. The purpose of this book is to educate and entertain. The author and publisher do not guarantee anyone following these techniques, suggestions, tips, ideas, or strategies will become successful. The author and publisher shall have neither liability nor responsibility to anyone with respect to any loss or damage caused, or alleged to be caused, directly or indirectly by the information contained in this book. Views expressed in this publication do not necessarily reflect the views of the publisher.

Cover Design: by Triv ilovedesignsbytriv@gmail.com

Printed in the United States of America
Keen Vision Publishing, LLC
www.publishwithKVP.com
ISBN: 978-1-955316-99-6

For my readers, may you press toward the mark for the prize of the high calling of God in Christ Jesus.
Philippians 3:14 (KJV)

TABLE OF CONTENTS

Introduction 11
Overcoming Word Curses 15
Are You Speaking Life or Death? 21
The Function of a Lie 27
The Root 31
Come Outta There 37
Comparison 43
I am a Lie Breaker 47
Affirmations 49

Acknowledgments 51
Meet the Author 55
Stay Connected 57

LIE
/lī/

noun

The thing that falsifies information.
The thing that produces inaccurate statements.
The thing that deliberately deceives.
The thing that intends to persuade from the truth.
The thing that misleads, misinforms detours,
perverts and deviates from the absolute truth.

INTRODUCTION

"Sticks and stones may break my bones, but words will never hurt me."
That, indeed, is a bold-faced lie.

-Davian Talley

As I reflect over my life and the experiences of others, I wish I knew this truth long ago. We live in a time where our self-images are often dictated by what we hear, see, and the opinions of others. Whether these opinions come from friends, family, social media, oneself, or television, they can lead a person down a path of living with entangled lies and wrestling with the spirit of comparison. I encourage you to self-reflect and begin to dismantle any lie that deviates from God's master plan for your life. It was not until I reflected and experienced the unconditional love of Christ that I began to decipher what was true or a lie.

Despite what others may say, what is God saying about you? Jeremiah 29:11 (NIV) reads, *"'For I know the plans I have for you,' declares the LORD, 'plans to prosper you and not to harm you, plans to give you hope and a future.'"*

Have you taken the time to find out the truth

about yourself? Could it be that you have been living a lie because of labels that were attached to you at an early age? Or maybe it's because of lies that were attached to you throughout your life experiences? Chances are you have dreamed of being successful, starting that business, reconnecting with family, finishing that college degree, marrying the love of your life, building that dream home, becoming debt free, or starting the ministry that God has placed on your heart. What else has God shown you in your dreams that you can't seem to reach because the lies you believe have you trapped? My hope is that this book will encourage you to stop being entangled in the web of lies in your life. I hope that you will develop the freedom and courage to believe the truth and that the absolute truth will set you free from yourself.

So if the Son sets you free, you will be free indeed.
John 8:36 (NIV)

Don't allow others' **ILLEGAL PERCEPTIONS** of you to determine **WHO YOU ARE.**

*Davian Talley
Don't Believe the Lie*

OVERCOMING WORD CURSES

An undeserved curse will be powerless to harm you. It may flutter over you like a bird, but it will find no place to land.

Proverbs 26:2 (TPT)

Words have the power to cut, damage, manipulate, control, and destroy one's mind, body, and soul if allowed through belief. Words are capable of sticking with you for a lifetime. It could be as simple as remembering someone calling you names and attaching labels to you based on their own agendas, insecurities, or perceived notions about you. I know this too well because I was teased and bullied throughout my adolescent years. Trust me, I can recall every negative word. I understand that bullies are ones that tease and taunt. They are usually judgmental and insecure and receive gratification from making someone else feel insignificant. Cowards. I know that now, but back then, I did not realize it. The words did hurt, and at times, it seemed as though some of the words began to take root in me physically and mentally. Once your mind gets accustomed to hearing something consistently, you begin to live it out mentally. It manifests into your soul and can begin to take root. I finally had to come to grips with the word curses that were hovering over my life, my decision-making, my actions, and my self-perception by tracing it back to the unstable root. Somehow, I had begun to entertain every lie that was ever imposed on me: fat, ugly, lame, gay, unintelligent, not cool, and the list goes on and on.

The moment I realized I no longer believed the lies of torment, something changed. I spoke back to the lies with confidence. I changed my mind by repeating the actual truth, according to what God said about me, and that's when liberation sprang forth. All I could think was, *"Lies, lies, you cannot hold me down."* I refused to allow the lies to muzzle my mouth any longer. I hope that you can find the courage to speak to and dismantle the webs of lies in your life. Sure, it may cause you to fret and bring your life some discord, but it will not derail God's intended purpose and power for your life.

How to overcome the word curses:
- Reject it.
- Reverse the curse by speaking against it.
- Send it back and renew your mind daily.
- Speak God's Word over your life.
- Be reminded that you have power over the curse.
- Speak against and rebuke what you know is not of God.
- Love yourself.
- Don't be so critical of yourself.
- Know that God wants you to know the truth.

- Know that you deserve to know the truth.
- We lack knowledge because we don't search for it, so read the scriptures.

My people are destroyed for lack of knowledge.
                                        Hosea 4:6 (KJV)

- Meditate on the scriptures day and night.
- Surround yourself with people who agree with your absolute truth.

Seeds of negative words can lead you down a path of low self-esteem, self-doubt, and insecurities. Be mindful of what you speak and whom you allow to speak into your life. You must know that not everyone is a dream pusher; many are dream stealers and killers. The sooner you know the difference, the sooner you can separate the two. Go ahead and brace yourself because distinguishing the two may sometimes separate you from family and some of your closest associates. Notice that I said associates instead of friends. Your true friends should always encourage you to thrive.

WARNING: Your genuine supporters may not be the closest people to you. You will be all right the sooner you accept that.

Do your WORKS *heal* or hurt?

Davian Talley
Don't Believe the Lie

ARE YOU SPEAKING LIFE OR DEATH?

Death and life are in the power of the tongue: And they that love it shall eat the fruit thereof.

Proverbs 18:21 (ASV)

This is something to think about. People talk so much throughout the day, whether it is to our family, co-workers, friends, or strangers. Our cell phones stay busy all day with social media, FaceTime, texting, and more. There is a plethora of platforms to express yourself, saying anything you want. Here is the big question: what are you really saying?

What is coming from your mouth? What if we could keep track of what we say all day and every day? That would be pretty scary honestly. It is highly important that we make sure we speak life into people, including ourselves.

You would think that words would not carry that much weight, but the truth is they carry a lot of weight. In fact, our words may be heavy enough to lift someone out of despair. Imagine if your words encouraged someone to follow their dreams, prevented someone from committing suicide, or led someone to Christ.

We have even noticed that political campaigns tend to use words and accusations to demean and ridicule their opponents as the world watches.

Children tend to recite words they hear from home. Honestly, their conversations are not always charming either. It is imperative that we daily exercise the intent to create and carefully encourage and not condemn. We should uplift and not tear down; we should speak life and not speak death. Your words might just bring a river of possibilities to someone that is drowning. So what are you saying now that you have their attention? Remember that your words of kindness, love, edification, exhortation, and encouragement may cause someone to reverse the lie over their lives.

> *But he who prophesies speaks edification and exhortation and comfort to men.*
> 1 Corinthians 14:3 (NKJV)

During middle school, I was judged for being overweight and was called "fat" consistently. Sure, I could have put the fork down at times and exercised; however, the more I would hear such slander, the more I would agree with it. I began to look in the mirror daily and speak over myself about being "fat" and "ugly." At times, the thoughts of starving my body just to lose weight came to mind. There was a great plan from the enemy in addition to this. The spirit of gluttony began to take over; there was a heavy desire to eat, eat, and eat some more. This bad habit was a void to fill the hurt and pain of the word curses I was accepting. Hurt became my place of comfort. My mindset was, *"If I am fat to others, then fat I shall become."* These were the thoughts the enemy fed my young mind daily. I was beginning to accept defeat instead of fighting back.

Gluttony and low self-esteem remained in my life until the end of high school. I took the initiative to start exercising and attempted to develop a better lifestyle. Sounds good right? The problem was that my heart and mind were not in the right place. I decided to make lifestyle changes but only to please others. I did it to hear, *"You look skinny"* or *"You're in shape."* It's possible to decide to be great and only do it for the opinions and approval of others. The more you do things for other people's acceptance, the longer you will stay in a box of untapped potential. It took a while for my mind to realize that I didn't deserve to be treated in that manner. I shouldn't have accepted the word curses. If I could go back and speak to my adolescent self, I'd say, *"Don't ever be afraid to be yourself, and never allow the opinions of others to drive you to change for them. Change comes from within. Do it for yourself."*

How many times have we discredited the work of God because of insecurity, comparison, or other people's views of us? I had started to believe the lies as I rehearsed them in my mind and my ears after I heard them. In actuality, there was nothing wrong with me. If God made us to be a masterpiece, then that includes every blemish, birthmark, and body deformation. It all contributes to His plan of making us unique. The more we complain and hate what was given to us by Him, the more we tell Him that His work is not good.

For we are God's masterpiece. He has created us anew in Christ Jesus, so we can do the good things he planned for us long ago.

Ephesians 2:10 (NLT)

DESTINY:

the PREDESTINED PLACE God has ordained *for you.*

Davian Talley
Don't Believe the Lie

THE FUNCTION OF A LIE

The function of a lie's assignment is to kill, steal, and destroy your God-ordained purpose.

Davian Talley

I repeat: The function of a lie's assignment is to kill, steal, and destroy your God-ordained purpose. There comes a time when you must realize the function of a lie was always to derail you from the absolute truth for your life. Think about it: if you believe a lie the enemy has hovering over you, it will take you longer to arrive at the door of destiny.

If you continue to believe the lie of fear, you will never overcome it and accomplish all God intended for you to do. It seemed I took the long route to get to my truth and destination. I can remember being confused and bound with fear and unforgiveness after college. I was exiting a season where I had believed so many of the lies that manifested in my life. I was having an identity crisis.

An identity crisis is any crisis that creates a wrestle with your DNA in Christ.

–Davian Talley

I was wrestling between who I tried to be based on past lies, who I thought I wanted to become, who the world dictated I should be, and who God said I was. I felt as though I was walking in the wilderness. Even though I was surrounded by people, I still felt alone. Have you ever been exiting one season and approaching a new one, but it seemed that you were stuck between the two? Lies will often keep you in a repetitive cycle. The lie's rhythm is like a merry-go-round; it keeps spinning you in the same cycle. It does not plan on stopping for you; you must decide enough is enough and leap off with faith. You may find yourself trying to get off, but fear will not allow you to leap. It was not until I leaped with faith that I landed on truth. The truth is that God had been preparing me for this very moment. **Be encouraged: what seems like isolation may just be separation for the preparation for God's glory.**

Therefore, if anyone is in Christ, the new creation has come: The old has gone, the new is here!

2 Corinthians 5:17 (NIV)

I AM
WHO I AM
BECAUSE OF
THE GREAT I AM

Davian Talley
Don't Believe the Lie

THE ROOT

Don't be afraid to go back to the root. The very thing that hurt you may heal you and someone else.

Davian Talley

Every plant has a root. The root provides anchorage and allows food to be absorbed for nutrients to help the plant grow stronger. Much like a plant, every lie has a growth process. The lie starts off as a seed, disguised as a thought or idea. In the beginning stage of a lie, it is used to create confusion and deceive the mind, the battlefield. When this seed is accepted into the mind, it goes from a simple thought to a new belief. Although the seed was a lie to begin with, it has now become an entrapment for one to use as their new belief system about themselves or something else. Understand that this is how simple it is to believe something. The enemy uses this method daily to destroy God's people. Not only does the enemy use this, but *people* will also use this against weaker minded individuals to manipulate and control their lives.

It is critical to not only understand how roots of a lie grow deeper in people but to also understand the harvest that comes along later. Yes, harvest time will soon come for the lies we allow to download in our lives. If you believe a lie, you will speak the lie, then the lie will be lived out by you. Our belief system shapes our future, eventually showing as a consistent lifestyle.

I'm sure we can all recall a time where we started consistently saying or doing something that was out of our norm. We start to ask ourselves, *"Where is this coming from?" or "When did I start this habit?"* This is the best time to evaluate yourself and your life, which requires serious and intentional soul searching. You must get to the root. The root is what is continuing to give life to most of our actions, thought processes, and habits whether good or bad. In this case, the lie is the root that needs to be dealt with.

Our problem in life is that most of us do not want to go through the process of revisiting what truly hurt us to begin with. Well, the question you must ask yourself is, *"Am I really ready to end this bad relationship?"* Yep, most of us have either been in a nasty relationship with these lies or are still entangled by them today. Getting to the root of these lies is not easy as at all. It takes courage, transparency, and honesty with God and yourself. Don't be discouraged because what gets revealed will get healed. Having the root of the lie exposed, coupled with the truth of why it was believed by you will soon bring healing. Just like digging up any plant to remove or relocate it, it is not the easiest. Why? It's because of the root; dealing with roots can get tough. Just like any root that grows over long periods, the root of a lie becomes deeply embedded in the ground. You may have realized your roots may be deeper than what you expected them to be, but you must remain consistent and confident to be free from the roots of the lie.

GOD IS WAITING ON YOU

Davian Talley
Don't Believe the Lie

COME OUTTA THERE

For whoever wants to save his life will lose it. But whoever loses his life for My sake will find it.

Matthew 16:25 (DLNT)

Coming out of a lie will never be an effortless process. It's indeed just that: a process. I will always remember a quote my pastor states from time to time. *"Once you are exposed to something, you can no longer be unexposed from it."* When you are exposed to truth, what was old should not be the desire anymore. The longer you believe a lie, the longer it will bear fruit of its own. You never want to be in a place where the opportunity for the lie to be destroyed presents itself but you either hesitate or allow fear to grip you away from freedom. I remember plenty of times when God was giving me the opportunity to be free from a lie that once had me trapped. I chose to listen to the lie and not God. Because of my disobedience, God stepped in and destroyed everything around me that would continue to feed or resemble the lie.

Since our flesh is always at war with the spirit man, we must daily remind ourselves that who we once were is no longer our present-day reality. Withal, this means you must be ready to handle life with a made-up mind and a desire to fight. Some of us may have a long history record of fighting people lol. Keep that same energy. Instead of fighting a person, aim for the spiritual things in high places.

> For we wrestle not against flesh and blood,
> but against principalities, against powers,
> against the rulers of the darkness of this world,
> against spiritual wickedness in high places.
> Ephesians 6:12 (KJV)

These powers were created with intent to work against you while fueling those lies to work in your life.

Come out of the lie, I decree!

As you prepare for a fight against the lies that have kept you bound, the following can help you prepare to war:

- Make sure you remember and recite the declarations and affirmations God has already spoken over you.
- Fighting looks like echoing to yourself that if you backslide into the lies, remember that grace is waiting to greet you back into the place of secure assurance. It happens to a lot of us in the process.
- Fighting the lie is embracing the new you the season brought and not being afraid to accept him/her.
- Fighting the lie is not being afraid of the future and what it will hold.

Fighting the lie is not taking the time to ponder on the past and lock into the illusion it sometimes brings. Now is your time to walk into new life. One cannot experience this new life because a lie will automatically kick you out and disqualify you for the next.

BELIEVE *in yourself*

LOVE *what God placed in you*

Davian Talley
Don't Believe the Lie

COMPARISON

Comparison will keep you locked in a box that you were never called to be in.

-Davian Talley

When it comes to believing a lie, comparison is one of those silent killers. It's something that seems very harmless, yet we tend to do this every day: compare, compare, compare. There's money, beauty, social media followers, popularity, spiritual gifts, and more; you name it, we compare it. What we tend to forget or may not know is that comparison will move us away from our identity. It is imperative to know who we are, always. Whenever we lose sight of who we are, we find reasons to compare our lives to something or someone else. Why? It is simply because we are not secure in what we have or who we are. People often use comparison as a model with hopes that it will set a standard for their lives. This troubled concept comes to feed our insecurities and make us view everything we do as *"never good enough."* If not handled correctly, comparison will cause us to give up on everything we once wanted and dreamed of.

If not quickly dismantled, comparison has the power to lead people into a false narrative and engulfment of lies. Please understand that comparison is not always a bad thing. If examined with caution, it can be a healthy tool for living a better life. The problem exists when we demean ourselves by using the comparison to focus on the negatives in our lives. Do not allow what you compare to determine your worth. You are already enough in God's sight. Have you given yourself grace today? Yes, you deserve to give yourself grace to understand that the process is ongoing. What is for you is for you. Remember that everyone is created and rewarded differently. Lastly, believe in yourself. Lies formed from comparison are only weakened by your act of belief. Do not be fooled by what you see. Get out of the habit of discounting who you are based on the outward appearance of others. *"People judge by outward appearance, but the LORD looks at the heart"* 1 Samuel 16:7 (NLT).

Each one should test their own actions. Then they can take pride in themselves alone, without comparing themselves to someone else, for each one should carry their own load.

Galatians 6:4-5 (NIV)

THE
LIE
ENDS
NOW

Davian Talley
Don't Believe the Lie

I AM A LIE BREAKER

The lie breaks once you break it.

-Davian Talley

Once you are aware that the lies placed on you were created to prevent you from achieving greatness, you will understand that you were created to break the lies. As I continued to grow, I found a deeper level of appreciation for what I went through. It challenged me to know that every lie and false reality was well worth it in the end. For every test, there is a lesson; after you've learned the lesson, a blessing awaits. Understand that you are not the only one in this world battling these different fabrications. If you are breathing, there will always be a series of battles where you will have to defeat the lie by not believing in it. It is a never-ending fight for your belief and perspective. Your former self will visit periodically to see if you are still open for business. In this case, you should never be available or open to receive those former things, which include the lies, habits, thoughts, and opinions. I declare over you that this is your moment in time to break free. The lie breaks once you break it.

Once you determine that the lie you believed is not beneficial for your life, it has no choice but to fall off of you in that moment. I'll leave you with these final takeaways.

You are more powerful than you think. The lie is only as strong and powerful as you make it. Change your perspective and self-perception. Do not look at yourself in the lens of that particular lie; view yourself from the lens of truth. Extend grace to yourself. Know that you are not perfect, nor will you ever be. Understand that all beautiful things go through a process to get to the final stage. Remember the process of a caterpillar to a butterfly. You were built for this. Get back in the game. Don't give up on yourself or the things you're called to do. The lie is only a distraction to get you off course. Now repeat these last words out loud with as much confidence and assurance as possible: I am a lie breaker.

AFFIRMATIONS

I am not hard to love.
I am fearfully and wonderfully made.
I have everything I need to be successful.
I lack nothing.
I am the head and not the tail.
I am a lender and not the borrower.
I know the heights I have access to regardless of limitations from others or i set for myself.
I am not crazy but I am crazy enough to believe in myself.
I am unstoppable, nothing can bring me down unless I allow it.
I have the power within to control my thoughts, actions, and emotions.
I deserve better so I choose to live better.
What I speak shapes my world for tomorrow, I will watch what comes out of my mouth.
I will filter what enters my ears.
I will monitor what is rehearsed in my mind.

DON'T BELIEVE THE LIE

I am not weak, I am strong.
I am healed.
My outcome is not determined by the opinions of others.
I am enough. Period.
I am capable of achieving what I desire.
I am somebody.
What is for me will not miss me, I will be patient in the process.
I am not rejected, I am loved.
I am one of a kind.
Fear is a liar, I believe in myself.
I am worthy of having the best in life.
I respect myself enough to have boundaries.
I will not conform to the opinions of others.
I am grateful to have what I have and I will not compare my life to others.

ACKNOWLEDGMENTS

Where exactly do I start?

First, I thank God for allowing me this opportunity to share this book with the world. I am absolutely nothing without Him!

I am extremely grateful for a lot of people who have been in my reach to help me through various seasons of hardship and success.

To my parents, family, and mentors: There is no back up crew like you all. I could go on and on but with much appreciation, Thank you. You've shaped me into the man I am today, and I am forever grateful.

Corey Battle, I honor you and truly appreciate you for always being there from the start. Words could never explain how much I honor you and thank you for accepting me through the ups and downs. You are the reason I never gave up and I am grateful.

Briana Tanner, your consistent humor and amazing spirit is the reason I still stand today. I used to underestimate the power in laughter but being around you taught me not second guess the importance of it. Thank you for being the light and showing me that the press is indeed necessary.

Deysha Garner, you are a person I could never get tired of, even though I get tired of your foolery! Thank you for believing in me and always giving me the clearance to always be myself.

Benjamin Mastin, man, you are a silent killer. Some people you run into and never expect for them to grow on you fast. You are that type of person. Thank you for being so supportive and investing into my life.

Yolanda Toney, you've been a great supporter and overall amazing human being. You have always been so consistent, nice, and welcoming. Your consistent push and motivation are the reasons why I'm on fire for the next.

To my spiritual leader and supreme Pastor, Pastor Adrian Davis. I cannot thank you enough for the pour, the teaching, equipping, and the covering. You have opened my eyes to a lot that I never thought I would see. To Pastor Brandon Clack, thank you for seeing my value even when I didn't.

I love you all truly.

To the reader, I appreciate your willingness to support this book. I pray you have been encouraged, inspired, and transformed from the message given in this book. My deepest desire is for someone to be changed forever after encountering this! I have no doubt you will be successful and determined to make a big

ACKNOWLEDGMENTS

difference in your life that will change your today for a better tomorrow.

MEET THE AUTHOR

Davian Talley is a born leader, speaker, Influencer, and a creative strategist to the world. He is a native of Huntsville, AL. Davian has always had a passion for the arts. He was born into a musical and writing family therefore, sharing his gift of music and writing is not a surprise. He has felt compelled to inspire and impact the lives of others through ministry, music, and his business endeavors. He has learned the significance of sharing his talents and gifts with others.

He received his Bachelor of Arts Entertainment Business at the University of North Alabama in Florence. Davian is currently the CEO of Devoted Enterprises, LLC. which oversees various avenues of entertainment and talent.

Davian has sensed at a young age that he would be instrumental in leading others and using his voice to inspire others. He has learned the significance of sharing his talents, and gifts with others. Therefore, he chose to compile his inspiration in *Don't Believe The Lie* in hopes to encourage others to always seek the absolute truth of who and what God has called them to be.

STAY CONNECTED

Thank you for reading, *Don't Believe the Lie.* Davian looks forward to connecting with you. Here are a few ways you can connect with the author and stay updated on new releases, speaking engagements, products, and more.

FACEBOOK Davian Talley
INSTAGRAM @daviandewayne
WEBSITE www.daviantalley.com
EMAIL info@daviantalley.com

STAY CONNECTED

www.ingramcontent.com/pod-product-compliance
Lightning Source LLC
Chambersburg PA
CBHW070107100426
42743CB00012B/2681